SARAH ROYCE AND THE
AMERICAN WEST

**HISTORY
EYEWITNESS**

EDITED WITH AN INTRODUCTION
AND ADDITIONAL MATERIAL BY
JANE SHUTER

RSVP
**RAINTREE
STECK-VAUGHN**
PUBLISHERS
The Steck-Vaughn Company

Austin, Texas

Published by Raintree Steck-Vaughn Publishers, an imprint of Steck-Vaughn Company

Design by Green Door Design Ltd., map by Jeff Edwards

Library of Congress Cataloging-in-Publication Data

Royce, Sarah, 1819-1891.
    Sarah Royce and the American West / edited with an introduction and additional material by Jane Shuter.
        p.   cm. — (History eyewitness)
    Based on: A frontier lady / by Sarah Royce.
    Includes index.
    ISBN 0-8114-8286-3
    1. Royce, Sarah, 1819-1891 — Diaries — Juvenile literature.   2. Women pioneers — West (U.S.) — Diaries — Juvenile literature.   3. Pioneers — West (U.S.) — Diaries — Juvenile literature.   4. West (U.S.) — History — 1848-1860 — Juvenile literature.   5. Frontier and pioneer life — West (U.S.) — Juvenile literature.
    [1. Royce, Sarah, 1819-1891 — Diaries.   2. Pioneers. 3. Women — Biography.   4. Diaries.   5. Frontier and pioneer life — West (U.S.).   6. West (U.S.) — History.] I. Shuter, Jane.   II. Royce, Sarah, 1819-1891. Frontier lady.   III. Title.   IV. Series.
F593.R69   1996
978'.02'092 — dc20
[B]   95-19117
                                                      CIP   AC

Acknowledgments
The publishers would like to thank the following for permission to reproduce photographs:

Amon Carter Museum, Fort Worth, Texas: pp.30, 35
Barnaby's Picture Library: p.45
Bridgeman Art Library/Yale University Art Gallery: p.17
California State Library: pp.33, 37
Denver Public Library: p.9
The Gerald Peters Gallery, Santa Fe, New Mexico: p.6
Idaho State Historical Society: p.41
Jefferson National Expansion Memorial/National Park
    Service: p.20
Montana Historical Society, Helena: p.42
National Cowboy Hall of Fame: cover and pp.14, 26
Peter Newark's Western Americana: pp.22, 25, 29
Smithsonian Institution: p.19
The Thomas Gilcrease Institute of American History and
    Art, Tulsa, Oklahoma: p.12
University of Michigan Museum of Art, Bequest of Henry
    C. Lewis: p.10

The cover photograph shows *Emigrants Crossing the Plains* by Alfred Bierstadt, 1867.

Every effort has been made to contact copyright holders of material reproduced in this book. Any omissions will be rectified in subsequent printings if notice is given to the publisher.

Printed in China
Bound in the United States
1 2 3 4 5 6 7 8 9 0 LB 99 98 97 96 95

Note to the Reader

In this book some of the words are printed in **bold** type. This indicates that the word is listed in the glossary on pages 46–47. The glossary gives a brief explanation of words that may be new to you.

CONTENTS

Introduction

Sarah Royce

Sarah Royce was born in Stratford-upon-Avon, England, in 1819 and brought to the United States when she was just six weeks old. Her husband was also born in England, in 1812, and was taken to Canada as a baby. Sarah was brought up in New York State. Her parents were wealthy enough to afford to send her to school and college, and she placed a great deal of value on education all of her life. In New York State she met and married Josiah Royce — they had a daughter, Mary, in 1847. In 1849 they joined the gold rush to California. In California, while moving from place to place, they had two more girls, Harriet then Ruth. In 1855, while living in Grass Valley, they had a son, named Josiah, after his father. It was at her son's request that Sarah Royce turned her brief "Pioneer Journal" into a book that could be easily read and understood by everyone. It is this book, *A Frontier Lady*, on which our edition is based. Sarah Royce and her husband returned to San Francisco in 1866, where she lived until she died in the late 1890s.

The Forty-niners

The Forty-niners is the name given to those people who set off to find gold in California, in 1849. They were followed, in the 1850s, by many other gold-seekers, but 1849 was the year in which the gold rush really began. Those who started it have a special place in its history; indeed, San Francisco has named its professional football team after them!

Gold was first found in Sutter's Creek on January 24, 1848, by James Marshall and John Sutter. Once it was confirmed that this was not an isolated find, people flocked to California. Some went by ship, around the coast of South America. This was the longest route but in many ways the safest. Others took a ship but chose to shortcut across the **isthmus** that divides North and South America, from Chagres to Panama. This seemed quicker, but the journey across the isthmus was dangerous, and as the wait for a ship out of Panama was long, it was not as short as it seemed. Most people went overland. The overland route had the advantage of being the shortest way and the cheapest. It was also the most dangerous. The dangers of the journey were followed by the hardships of actually mining for gold. Many men who had given up good jobs in the East and traveled west in the hopes of getting rich quick were badly disappointed. Yet not that many went home. There were just enough people who did get rich to make them hang on.

The gold rush in California finally fizzled out. People settled for farming instead. But "gold fever" continued to strike in the United States and Canada, dragging people to more and more inhospitable places, including Alaska, in the 1890s.

4

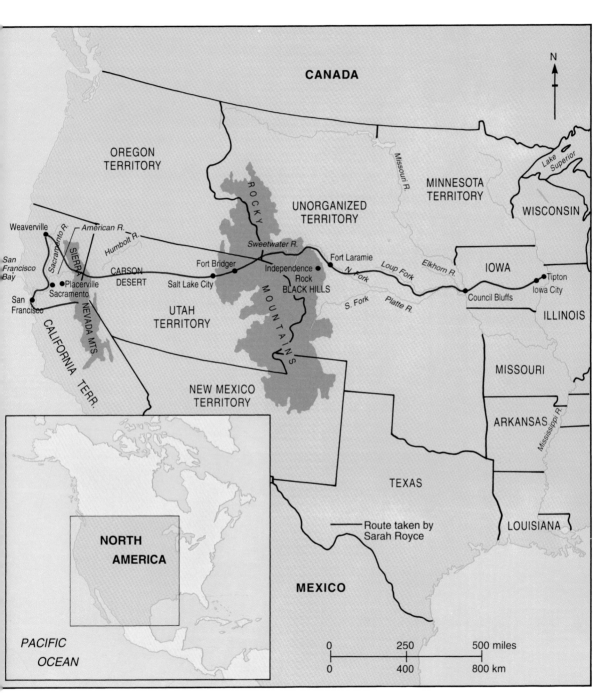

CANADA

OREGON
TERRITORY

ROCKY

UNORGANIZED
TERRITORY

MINNESOTA
TERRITORY

Lake
Superior

WISCONSIN

Weaverville

San
Francisco
Bay

San
Francisco

American R.

Sacramento R.

SIERRA

CARSON
DESERT

Humbolt R.

Sweetwater R.

Fort Bridger

Salt Lake City

Independence
Rock
BLACK HILLS

Fort Laramie

N. Fork

Loup Fork

Elkhorn R.

Missouri R.

IOWA

Tipton
Iowa City

Placerville
Sacramento

NEVADA MTS.

UTAH
TERRITORY

M
O
U
N
T
A
I
N
S

S. Fork

Platte R.

Council Bluffs

ILLINOIS

CALIFORNIA TERR.

NEW MEXICO
TERRITORY

MISSOURI

ARKANSAS

Mississippi R.

NORTH
AMERICA

TEXAS

LOUISIANA

—— Route taken by
Sarah Royce

PACIFIC

OCEAN

MEXICO

0		250		500 miles
0		400		800 km

N

This map shows the places that
Sarah Royce mentions in her story.
We cannot show the exact route that
she followed, but the route we have
given is likely to be quite accurate.

5

CHAPTER 1

Setting Out

Pioneers, *painted by William Ranney in 1850. This was the sort of wagon that Sarah Royce would have traveled in. The wooden bar and straps holding the two oxen pulling the wagon together is the yoke. "Yoke" is also used to mean the animals who are working in pairs wearing it. These emigrants also have at least one other wagon in the party and at least one horse to ride. It is possible to get some idea of how the prairie stretches out flat and featureless for miles.*

On the last day of April 1849, we left the village near the Mississippi River, where we had rested, and began our journey to California. Our **outfit** was a covered wagon, well-loaded with **provisions** and such goods for sleeping, cooking, etc., as we had been able to find. We were guided in our choice by Frémont's *Travels* and suggestions, often conflicting, of those who, like ourselves, utter strangers to camping life, were heading for the "Golden Gate." Our wagon was drawn by three **yoke** of oxen and one yoke of cows, the cows only being used in the **team** part of the time. Their milk was to be a valuable part of our diet.

The morning was not very bright, but neither was it gloomy. It might rain, but then the sun might come out. I did not want to delay our departure any longer. So I seated myself in the wagon, my two-year-old, Mary, was placed beside me, my husband and the other man of our little **party** started the team, and we were on our way. The day turned out not to be unpleasant. Our first noon lunch was eaten in front of the wagon, with the oxen **unyoked** and grazing nearby. The afternoon wore quietly away, and night was coming on. There was not a house in sight. Why did I look for one? I knew we were to camp, but surely there would be a few trees or a sheltering hillside against which to put our wagon? No, only the level **prairie** stretched out on each side of the way. I had anticipated this hour for months, yet not until it came did I realize the blank dreariness of it — and it was to be the same for weeks, even months. It was a chilling prospect, and my heart shrank from it.

I kept this to myself, and we were soon busy making things comfortable for the night. Our little Mary, happy as a lark all day, now fell fast asleep. At first, the oppressive sense of homelessness and an instinct of watchfulness kept me awake. But sleep came at last, then morning and with it the cowardly fit had gone away.

But the oxen and cows had gone away, too! It was late morning before they were rounded up and yoked to the wagon for our second day's journey. Travel was not easy. We encountered deep mud holes in which the wagon stuck fast. Worse than these were the sloughs — boggy patches covered with seemingly safe turf, which broke as the full weight of the wagon was on them, letting the wheels in up to the hubs, holding on so tightly that digging alone would not free them. In these cases, most of the contents of the wagon had to be unloaded, often in very muddy places, sometimes in the rain, for the men to heave the wagon out. Several times when we were busy doing this the cattle would wander off, and hours would be lost finding them. They were often lost in the morning anyway — they had to be turned loose to graze at night — the best traveling part of the day would be gone before we could move out. Some days the weather was so bad that we could not travel at all.

The rain was a problem in several ways. Not only did it keep us from traveling, but it also made the ground very soft. This meant that we were to find ourselves stuck more and more often. On the first Saturday, we spent a long, hard day traveling and arrived at the little town of Tipton, Iowa. We then figured out how far we had traveled. Our whole day's labor had covered just three miles! We spent our first Sunday in Tipton. The weather was still bad. In the town, we met up with three other wagons, and we all set out together. Three days later, when we reached the Cedar River, we found several others, all **bound** for California. It was good to have company, for we could help each other over hard places, saving much time. But the weather worsened. We now found that we had to travel all the time, even driving through the drenching rain.

We spent our second Sunday in Iowa City and on Monday morning crossed the Iowa River and continued on our way. Storms, bad roads, and swollen streams continued to hold us up nearly every day until we reached Council Bluffs. Indian Creek, when we reached it, was so swollen by the late rains as to be **impassable**. We had to remain there until the men built a bridge, which took them until the next day at noon, and it was lucky that by now we were part of a greater party.

TRAVEL GUIDES

Emigrants often set out into the unknown with little knowledge of what they were going to face — where to go, how to get there, or how to manage along the way.

Newspapers from the time published details of the route emigrants could follow, though they were seldom detailed enough to be of much use. The newspapers also listed the sorts of things they could usefully take with them. Many emigrants preferred the greater detail of a guidebook. These were published in great numbers with the discovery of gold in California in 1849. They were mostly written by people who had made the journey at least once.

In 1849 Joseph E. Ware's guide was recommended, as was a guide by Edwin Bryant who, in 1846, published the story of his journey west, called *What I Saw in California*. The book gave support to the guide. Other people chose to read accounts of trips west, like John C. Frémont's *Travels*. Frémont was an explorer who, in 1842, had already traveled to Oregon and written about that in detail. In 1846 he crossed into California, with a mapmaker, and published his story upon his return.

At Fort Des Moines, we met up with more wagons and heard bad news. **Cholera** was raging in Council Bluffs and at other crossing points on the Missouri. There were also stories of the difficulties in getting supplies, and that the animals of the settlers who were there before us had eaten up all the grass on the Great Plains. Yet we still went on and reached Council Bluffs one month and four days after we had set out. Here we found a city of wagons, some of which had been there many days waiting their turn to cross the river. But we were assured that the ferrymen were working as hard as possible, and that we would probably be across the river in a week or two.

We were a huge crowd of people, most of us strangers to each other, thrown together in new and inconvenient circumstances and with much to try our patience; yet, for the most part, good humor prevailed. Most of the crowd were men, farmers, mechanics, and the like. Some had their families with them, and their wagons were easily distinguished by the greater number of household articles they carried, which, in this long wait were taken out and disposed in a homelike way. At last our turn came to cross the river. On Friday, June 8, we ventured ourselves and all we owned onto a very unstable ferryboat and were slowly carried across the **turbid** and unfriendly looking Missouri. The cattle were "swum" across the river, driven in by the men on one side to find their way to the other. A few were driven by strong currents beyond the **flats** and were thereby lost, but most crossed safely. We had then to make a steep and dusty climb to the top of the **bluff** to find ourselves on an almost level plain, with only a tree or two in sight, except for a small clump of them to the southwest. Not very far from the river, we began to see the few scattered buildings of Trader's Point, the **Indian Agency** for this part of Nebraska.

There were very few houses. I remember only a blacksmith's shop and a pretty good-sized log house nearby. Yet this is where Omaha City very soon grew up. A slight accident seemed to have broken some part of the wagon, and we stopped at the blacksmith's for repairs. The other wagons moved on to camp for the night, over by the only visible clump of trees. As the blacksmith began work, the Indian Agent came and invited Mary and me into his house, the log house I mentioned earlier, to rest. I accepted the invitation, and his kindness extended to a good-sized dinner for all three of us and a rest and a social chat by his fireside. He then helped us into our wagon, directed us to the camping ground, some two miles away, and wished us good-night and good luck on our journey. From now on, I saw no house till we passed a few scattered dwellings at Fort Laramie [now Wyoming] and did not eat a meal in a house again until urged to do so, once only, by a hospitable **Mormon** woman, beside whose garden fence we placed our wagon during our stay in Salt Lake City.

From our arrival in Council Bluffs, we had been pestered by begging and **pilfering** Indians. You could not give anything — giving a thing to one would bring a dozen more to you. You had to keep them at a distance — not be friendly. Now there were even more of them. They had followed us all the way to the blacksmith's and dogged every other wagon, too. But the Indian Agent assured us that at night they would go; not to bed, for they had nothing of that sort, but to sleep in their camp among the sand hills. He assured us that they would not bother us as we made our way to the camping place, and they did not.

The men spent the next day organizing themselves. They made a system with a captain and subordinate officers, and rules and duties, all laid out. The few women in the company were busy cooking, washing, mending, and performing other domestic duties. Despite the disheartening reports that had been reaching us all, we were all still hopeful and determined to carry on. There were some who might have turned back, but they were urged on by others in their party who were more resolute — or rash! It was suggested that we should keep Sunday as a day of rest, but this was not agreed to. The lateness of the season — we were nearly the last to cross the Missouri — and the importance of keeping close to the larger **companies** ahead, meant we needed to set out the very next morning, Sunday, June 10. We rose early and packed and yoked up the wagons. When all was ready, the captain gave the command, "Roll out!" and we moved off in an orderly line. The sun shone brightly, and all looked hopeful. We made for the rolling hills between which our road lay.

People often joined up with each other for part of the way on a journey like this, often meeting at places where a stop was forced by the need to cross a river. Royce met up at Council Bluffs with people who were going to farm the West, as well as look for gold. People went on traveling west each year to look for farmland. That is what the settlers in the picture below intended to do. These settlers, photographed in 1867 in Utah, were Mormons. They were the family of Joseph Henry Byington.
*They are **left to right at the back**: Sarah (age 11), Elizabeth (age 6), Nancy (age 37), Nancy (age 17), Hannah (age 30).*
***Sitting, left to right**: Hyrum (age 8), Janette (age 2) and Joseph Henry (age 39). Mormons believed in having more than one wife.*
Joseph's wives were Nancy and Hannah.

CHAPTER 2

Indians and Cholera

The Attack on an Emigrant Train,
painted by Charles Wimar in 1856.
This picture was copied several
times by other artists and as prints
and etchings for book illustrations.
First encounters between white
people and the Indians were mostly
friendly, but relations deteriorated.
The Indians were affected by white
mistrust and white diseases. They
were also affected by white values.
Early settlers stress the Plains
Indians' view of themselves as
working with the land, not owning it.
But by 1850 there were several
tribes on the emigrant trail trying to
charge tolls. In fact, Indian attacks,
though dramatic, were the disaster
least likely to strike.

Suddenly many dark shapes appeared on the hills in the distance, on both sides of the road. What could they be? Were they the cattle of a larger company camped ahead? Or were we about to have our first sight of buffalo about which we had heard? As we drew near, the shapes proved to be hundreds of Indians, ranged on either side of the roadway. A group came forward; we halted, and the captain and several other men went to meet and **parley** with them. It turned out that they were in the habit of gathering a certain sum per head for every emigrant passing through this part of the country, which they claimed as their own. The men of our party talked over the demand of the Indians. Our men finally resolved that theirs was an unreasonable demand, as the land belonged to the United States, and the red men had no right to stop us. The Indians were told that we intended to move on without paying a dollar. They were further warned that if the Indians tried to stop them, they would open fire with all of their rifles and revolvers.

At the captain's word of command, all the men then armed themselves with every weapon they could—revolvers, knives, and hatchets glittered on their belts. Rifles and guns bristled on their shoulders. The drivers raised their long whips high and called to the animals to move off. At once we were moving between long but not very compact rows of half-naked redskins, many of them well armed, others with few weapons. All of them wore on their faces expressions of sullen disappointment, mingled with half-defiant scowls that suggested that they were considering night attacks in the future, when they would have the advantage of darkness and **thickets** for cover. For the present, however, they had evidently made up their minds to let us pass, and we soon lost sight of them.

But another enemy, unseen and unheard, was advancing on us and struck our wagon first. The oldest of the men who had joined us complained of intense pain and sickness and soon had to lie down in the wagon, which being quite large, had room for quite a comfortable bed in the space behind the seat where Mary and I sat. Soon he was overcome by terrible **spasms**; the captain was called, and he called a halt. The sick man was given medicine, which seemed to help. We had heard from some horsemen that there were others ahead of us camped at the Elkhorn River, who had a doctor among them. We made him as comfortable as we could and pressed on. When we reached the camp, we found the doctor, who said the disease was Asiatic cholera. We did all we could for him, considering our position, but to no avail — he was dead within two or three hours.

We all realized that, as we had been in close contact with him for several hours, we had been exposed to **contagion**. Our wagon and all it contained needed to be disinfected. Some of the people in the camp had tents as well as wagons, and one of these was provided for us, with a cot bed and other conveniences until our things could be disinfected. I will never forget that Sunday night. I refused to lie down, for apart from Mary, there was only space for one other to lie down and only coverings for one, too. My husband had been on guard the night before and working hard all day, so I insisted that he rest. I sat up and tried to sleep. But a storm blew up. The wind moaned, and the rain fell constantly.

Morning came at last. In the early dawn, we buried the old man. Then came the work of cleaning out the wagon, washing the bedding, sunning and airing everything; luckily the storm was over, and the sun was shining. Before we had half done, the other companies began to cross the river. The wagons and people went over on rafts, and the cattle were "swum." By early afternoon, we were all across. The next Wednesday morning, June 13, we were struck by the most terrible storm we had yet experienced, with thunder, lightning, and a tearing wind. Luckily, although the rain got into the wagons, our food and clothing stayed mostly dry. The next morning, just three days since we had buried the old man, two more of the group fell ill with the same disease. Before night fell, one man was dead. A heavy gloom hung around us. What if my husband should die, and Mary and I should be left in the wilderness? Or if I should die, leaving Mary motherless? Or worse, if we should both die and leave her an orphan among strangers in a land of savages? I was stricken by these thoughts. Then I prayed to God, committing us all to his care, and felt much better. The second of the two men began a slow recovery. From that time on, there were no more cases of cholera among us, though we heard from groups that camped near us that they had been affected, too.

DISEASE

There were some years when the emigrant trail suffered a lot of sickness and other years where there was very little. In the early 1840s, there was very little sickness, but the gold rush years were plagued with cholera outbreaks. Cholera was a disease that caused serious diarrhea and vomiting. It was usually carried in water that was not pure and could easily be fatal — particularly where there was no access to fresh water or medical help. It spread rapidly, especially among large groups of emigrants who had to wait in one place for any length of time — at a river crossing, for instance. It was more likely to be fatal if those who were sick were not given time to rest and recover before going on.

Chapter 3

Crossing the Plains

California Crossing; South Platte River, *painted by William Henry Jackson in the 1850s. Notice the cattle being swum across. The wagon in the front bears the slogan "Bill of the Woods Ho for Idaho you Bet." Many wagons had slogans painted on them. Some were brief and to the point: "Gold or a Grave," others were more wordy: "Blest are those that expect nothing, for they will not be disappointed." Slogans were useful for judging the flow of wagons. If a wagon's passengers saw mostly the same slogans as they traveled, then it was keeping pace with the rest. If the slogans kept changing, then either the wagon was pulling ahead, or worse, falling behind.*

On the evening of Saturday, June 16, we arrived at the crossing of the Loup fork of the Platte River. Here we found two companies who had been camped for some days, waiting for the waters to go down so they could find a crossing place. The river bed here is, for miles, formed of **quicksand**; where teams cross in safety one day, there might be deep holes the next. The waters were high due to the rain; finding a place to cross was very dangerous. A man was drowned just before we came by going too quickly when nearly across. He stepped into a deep channel, where the rushing waters and sand soon swallowed him up.

On the third day, it was announced that the water had subsided enough for us to try to cross, though there was still an ugly current near the farther shore. On our side, there was shallow water for some way, over which the teams could pull a lightly loaded wagon to a sand island. Then the water was deeper and the current stronger; we would have to double the teams and use long ropes to help haul. It was important to move quickly, for the sands shifted so constantly that the bottom changed about every hour. The quickest way of working was to take two or three wagons to the island at a time; then, fastening all the cattle to one wagon with several men to drive, rush across the deeper stream and return for another. As fast as one standing place on the island was vacated, another wagon was driven over the shallower channel to take its place. It was quite exciting for the women and children to be drawn across, but startling when we felt the ground quiver under us as we went. The quivering was constant on the island; had we been forced to stay long, we would have sunk.

A few days after this, we had a new and unexpected experience — a cattle stampede. When we camped for the night, we always formed a **corral**, by placing the wagons to form a large circle. The **tongue** of the wagon dropped to the ground as the cattle came out, and the next wagon was backed over it, with just enough room for a person to step through. We left a gate-sized space between the first and last wagon and, at night, drove the cattle into the circle, fastening the "gate" with ox chains attached to the wheels of the wagons. About four in the morning of June 20, I woke to a light rain on the wagon top. Then there was a flash of lightning, followed by a strange rushing sound, which quickly became as loud as thunder. Our wagon, one half of the "gate," began to shake violently, then was lifted and thrown over on its side; there was a crash of breaking wheels and chains, and the rapid tramp of cattle passed into the distance. The other "gate" wagon had also been overturned. We were lucky the ox chains broke, or the wagons would have been trampled and us in them. One of our wheels was broken, and two on the other wagon. We had just entered an area the guidebooks said had no trees for nearly two hundred miles except one, marked as "The Lone Tree." The Captain gazed in despair and cried, "Three wheels broken all to pieces, and fifty miles from wood!" What was to be done? Luckily some men had been quick to ride after the cattle — they were gaining on the fastest, and some of the slow ones were already being brought back. But what of the wheels? Luckily one of the men was a blacksmith and had the tools and skills to make a repair with some boards used for a table, though it took till the end of the next day.

Emigrants Crossing the Plains, painted by Alfred Bierstadt in 1867. The picture is obviously intended to make the journey look peaceful and attractive; however, the bleached bones of long-dead animals are a reminder that crossing the Plains was not always as easy as it seems here. The emigrants are mainly farmers. This is shown by the numbers of sheep and cows, and the slogan, "For Oregon" on the wagon.

We were now within 100 miles of Fort Laramie and saw Laramie Peak in the distance, a cheering contrast to the flat plain. On the evening of July 9, we camped within three miles of the fort. We rested and let the cattle graze for two days, then crossed the Platte, passed the fort, and camped just beyond it. We then entered the Black Hills, and, on the morning of July 15, we passed Laramie Peak. At noon of the same day, we found a beautiful spot to stop, with a stream running through it. We did not hurry to set off again, so I was able to take Mary to play down by the stream.

The pleasant surroundings soon changed. There was little grass for the cattle; all that at the side of the trail had been eaten by those who had gone before. On the evening of July 17, we camped at Deer Creek. The younger men went to search for grazing for the cattle; the older ones stayed behind to guard the wagons. Some fifteen miles upstream the men found good grazing and kept the cattle there for two days, communicating with us by riders who were sent to and fro.

Soon after we resumed our journey, we had to cross the Platte again, to the north side. And now, once again, a terrific storm overtook us. Thunder, lightning, wind, hail, and rain poured down. The terrified cattle were taken from the wagons to the most sheltered spot we could find. It was hard to stop another stampede. A day or two after this, about July 23, we reached the Sweetwater River, which we were to follow to its head, knowing that then we would be at the top of the Rocky Mountains. On July 26, we reached Independence Rock, named so by Frémont and his men because they were here on July 4. It is a bare mass of rock, standing out entirely from the surrounding land. Another woman and I climbed it, with her boy and Mary.

On Sunday, July 29, the camp divided. Some of us decided to rest and held a social meeting, for prayer, reading, and singing, and the next morning, we set off much refreshed. From this time until we reached Salt Lake City, there were just two men, two women, and four children, the oldest about eight, in our company. We followed the river to its head, then made for Frémont's Peak. On August 4, we reached the South Pass of the Rocky Mountains. We were lucky to have clear directions, for here we might have lost our way. We took a long, last look east — after this the mountains would always block our view — then began to descend. Twice we met Indians, but they let us be. We overtook our earlier companions; indeed, we later reached Salt Lake City a whole day before them, despite our stopping every Sunday, which they did not.

MESSAGES

This party kept in touch when they split up by sending riders with messages to each other. Groups changed all the time; people fell back, caught up, joined other groups, and so on. In this case, they often left messages, either on paper or carved into wood or bone (sometimes even human skulls). They were then stuck into a stick or attached to a bush — even, if there was nothing else, a grave marker.

We now had to spend several days crossing the extreme northern end of the great Colorado Valley. Many of the springs were so strong with **alkali** as to be powerfully poisonous, and the grass around them was the same. One of our oxen died on the second day after entering this area, and we had to yoke up all the rest and travel all night so as to get to safer feed and water. On Saturday of that week, we camped at night at a place called Black Fork, where we rested for the Sunday. The next day we reached Fort Bridger, a rough log fort and one or two log huts. We got what information we could here about the best route to follow, and then continued on our way.

The next day, August 14, we crossed the dividing ridge between the Colorado Valley and the Great Salt Lake Basin. Here, in the Wasatch Mountains, our road was by far the most **precipitous**, and the scenery was by far the wildest that we had seen or passed through so far. At the highest point of the road, we were at an altitude of something like seven thousand and some hundred more feet. Looking up to the peak that towered above us on our left, we distinctly saw snow driving and eddying about in a strong wind. The clouds came down low enough for us to get some rain, but as we went down, we came out into hot sunshine again. The dust, which had been tiresome for some days, grew deeper and finer as we progressed, so at the entrance to the Great Salt Lake Valley it was like wading through a bed of fine ashes.

It was near sunset on August 18 when we got our first view of the Great Salt Lake, with its background of mountains. In the foreground there was a well-laid-out city, with snug-looking dwellings and gardens. The suddenness with which we came on it was startling. Our road, narrow and mountainous, suddenly opened out and led through an opening that was almost like an immense doorway without the top arch. We were suddenly on a small **plateau** some hundreds of feet above the valley; there was nothing to obstruct the view for miles. It is impossible to describe how the thin atmosphere made everything so distinct that distance seemed not to exist. From the plateau, we wound gradually down the mountainside to the plain, then into the city. We camped when we reached the plain, as night was almost fallen, and entered the city the next day.

At this point, almost all company organizations seemed to break up. Every party made such arrangements as seemed best to those in the same wagon. In many cases, even those owning teams and wagons together chose to separate here, selling up, dividing goods and money, and each going their own way. A few groups hurried on at once, but most stayed at least a few days to rest. There was a general selling out of tired cattle and buying in fresh.

Soon after we arrived, it was formally announced that a man, whose name I forget, an experienced traveler who had explored the area, would lead a company to California by a route far more southerly than the ones that emigrants had used up to this point. He said he would leave the city in a month, two at the most, and advised the new arrivals to rest, then to join his party. We discussed the matter and decided against going with him on a new route. We decided to follow the tried and tested trail, from Great Salt Lake west, by way of the Humbolt River and the Carson Desert to the Sierras.

The Mormons warned us this was not a good route. We would lose our cattle and die in the desert or, if we reached the Sierras, would be snowed in and die there instead. We heard the warnings, discussed them, and perversely decided to go anyway. We set off on August 30 — a solitary wagon, three yoke of oxen, two men, one woman, and a little child. We had just enough food to last us over the mountains, with little to spare. Our only guide from Salt Lake City consisted of two small sheets of notepaper, sewn together, entitled "Best Guide to the Gold Mines, 816 miles, by Ira J. Willis." It was all handwritten; there was at that time no printing press in the city. Willis had been to California and back the year before. The directions and descriptions of camping places seemed pretty definite until the lower part of Humbolt's River, when poor camping and scarce water were mentioned with discouraging frequency. From the sink of the Humbolt, it was confused and uncertain; indeed, the man who sold the guide to my husband advised him to get better directions from Mormons who would come the other way.

IRA J. WILLIS

Ira J. Willis produced a guide that Sarah Royce used in 1849. Willis had recently made the crossing with some Mormons with loaded wagons, so the guide contained the most up-to-date information for crossing to California. However, the guide was sketchy in places. It was the only one that the Royce party could get. Later, more thorough guides were brought out, including *An Emigrant's Guide* by B. H. Young and J. Eager, first available in 1850, and *A Mormon's Way-Bill to the Gold Mines,* first available in 1851.

A print of Great Salt Lake City, Utah, from a point very similar to the place from which Sarah Royce would have first seen it.

CHAPTER 4

Lost in the Desert

The man who accompanied us was quite old and not in perfect health. He was very anxious to reach California, but only had one ox and just enough food to feed himself if he got straight through. He offered to put the ox in our team to speed the last and most perilous stage of the journey. On the morning of September 11, we were moving along, with no living creature in sight save ourselves and our plodding team, when suddenly a party of Indians approached. We saw they were all armed. A group of them arranged themselves across the road, blocking our way. We were completely in their power. Their numbers and their arms were enough to destroy us in a moment. There was no hope, except in finding a reason to persuade them to let us go. I prayed to God for help, for there was no other. My husband met them with a calm and dignified air, talking to them calmly, though they did not understand him, or he them. Their behavior changed several times, strangely. They seemed confident and demanding, then puzzled, then angry, then they would seem to differ among themselves. They kept us for about an hour, when my husband announced, "I'm going to move on," and set us moving. Would they let us carry on? They argued, some threatening us with guns, others restraining them. They were still at odds when we turned a bend and lost sight of them. We expected that they would waylay us again, but time passed, and night fell. We passed a bad night waiting for an attack, but we never saw them again.

Two days later, we met some Mormons who had been gold hunting for the summer and were on their way home to Salt Lake City. We asked for directions for the latter part of the journey, and their leader gave us directions from the sink of the Humbolt, which he assumed we could reach, drawing them in the sand with his whip handle. He was an experienced traveler. He advised us to camp for a few days in the meadows by the desert, letting the cattle roam and graze freely and filling the wagon with hay to keep them going in the desert. He also advised us to fill everything we could with water, stopping every few hours in the desert to rest ourselves and the animals. If we did this, he said, we should reach the Carson River, on the other side of the desert, in about twenty-four hours. We felt more cheerful for good directions and advice. On Sunday, September 16, we reached the Humbolt River, which we followed for several days. On October 2, we reached the point at which the Humbolt disappeared, from where our Mormon friend had drawn his map. We looked in the guidebook, and this spoke of the sink being some ten miles further on, so we assumed, wrongly, that this was what our Mormon friend had really meant. "So," we thought when we camped on the night of October 2, "we are some twelve miles from the meadow. A start before first light will enable us to reach the meadows by midday." So we set off by moonlight and, as day dawned, began to look hopefully for signs of the meadows.

HELP ALONG THE WAY

Sarah Royce was lucky to find the eastward-bound Mormons so helpful. People who were headed east were often besieged by people going west asking for directions, even for news of good places to find gold, to eat, sleep, and so on.

When they were meeting parties of thousands of people, it was hard for those going east to stay polite. One group in 1850 simply kept their mules going as fast as possible past every group, calling out instructions as they passed by, answering some of the questions they were "peppered with," but refusing to stop and talk.

But we traveled all day without sight of them and realized there had been a mistake — we had traveled all day through the desert. We had missed the meadows, passing them before the day began! We were miles into the desert with the animals unfed, no food set by, and little water. We stopped, tied up the animals, and fell asleep, exhausted. We had a couple of straw mattresses, which in the morning we fed to the animals. We wasted almost the whole morning deciding what to do. We had to go back. Despite the fact that this would leave us short of food, we would never manage in the desert with no water beyond the first hour, and no food for the cattle. It was, indeed, uncertain that we would even make it back to the meadows. It was hard to go back. Go back, on a journey like this, in which every mile we had traveled had been a great labor, and only the knowledge that we were a step nearer kept us moving on! No steps ever seemed so heavy, so hard to take as those back to the meadows.

We had not been moving long, when we saw a cloud of dust, and saw wagons coming toward us from the meadows. We told them our story and asked if they could spare enough grass and water for us to go with them. They said it was out of the question. Their cattle were weak already, the season too far advanced. It would be throwing away their lives, with no certainty of saving ours; for once out in the desert, we would all be helpless together. They went their way, and we carried on toward the meadows, some fifteen miles away, where they assured us there was plenty of grass and water.

A camp of Paiute Indians, also called, "Digger Indians." The Indian woman has a baby strapped to her back. These Indians lived in the area between Great Salt Lake City and the Sierra Nevadas. It could have been men from a group like this that Sarah Royce came across. These Indians managed to scratch a living out of the area, mainly by living on roots and berries.

I was now so worried about the animals giving out that I would not ride, except for brief rests. I walked and kept close to the wagon for most of the way, but at one point, when dusk was falling, before we reached the meadows, I lost sight of the wagon completely for a while. We had to camp for the night and resumed our backward march the next morning. The cattle had only a mouthful of mattress left, and we finished the water in the little cask with breakfast. We had had no chance to cook lately and ate cold boiled rice, dried fruit, and hard biscuit for breakfast. I had no trouble keeping up with the team this morning. They were slow and weak, and so were we. I passed the morning in a daze, only coming to with a start when Mary cried for water. I gave her some and noticed that there were only a few swallows left. I muttered over and over to myself, "Let me not see my child die." Noon came, and the horned heads bowed lower, and the hooves trudged more slowly. Then, just as I was giving up hope, we reached the meadows. We spent the rest of the day resting. The animals ate, and we drank. The next day, the men cut and spread grass to dry for fodder, while I rearranged the wagon to make as much room as I could for this and find as many water containers as I could. I also cooked the food that we had, for we would not be able to cook in the desert.

A photograph of a prairie schooner from the time, now in a modern museum. Prairie schooners were much bigger than the wagon in which Sarah Royce traveled, and had much higher sides. They were able to carry far more than the Royce wagon. They were the earliest wagons to cross the Plains, carrying people who wanted to farm in the West.

Sunday we rested. Monday we loaded up. We felt the cattle needed another day grazing, but we dared not stay longer. We camped that night at the edge of the desert, and on October 9, at noon, we set off into the sea of sand; this time to cross it or die. By the time we stopped to eat at night, we had reached the place where we had decided to turn back before. As I had walked much of the afternoon, and knew I would have to walk again soon, I was persuaded to get into the wagon and sleep. But I only slept a few minutes. I was roused by the wagon stopping and the ox chain rattling, and I knew one of our cattle was dead. I looked out, and it was so, and the ox that he was yoked to looked to be in the same state soon. They had been the weak pair all along. Now we could only count on two yoke. How long would they last? I refused to ride again. It was night, but the moon was not up yet. We could see, only too plainly, the bodies of dead cattle lying here and there on both sides of the road. There were more and more; then we came across two or three wagons.

At first we thought we were overtaking a moving group, but there was no sign of life as we drew near. We lit our candles and examined the scene. Everything indicated a complete breakdown and a hasty flight. Some yokes and chains had gone, indicating that the surviving animals had been taken on, with what few possessions they could carry. The things had all been rummaged through as if in search of essentials. We went on and found that what we had considered an exceptional misfortune was quite common — we came across several wagons in a similar state, at shorter and shorter intervals. We pressed on, resting and eating in snatches. Then we found some huge wagons, tall as a house, the kind called prairie schooners. We looked into the biggest of them. Hanging from the beams inside we found two **sides** of good bacon, which we took with us. These wagons, like all the others we had passed, were surrounded by hastily turned out boxes. There were also lots of pretty boxes, full of brooches and the like, from which we concluded that the wagons had belonged to merchants who were hauling goods to California to sell. Now morning was coming, and we hoped to soon see the river. For two or three weary hours after sunrise, we saw nothing but desert. The cattle had had the last of the water before daylight, and the last of the hay. I had spent so long staring at the horizon, desperate for a change that, when it came, I was not sure that I saw it. There was what seemed to be a dark line on the horizon. I asked my husband what he thought it was. "I think it is the trees along the river," he said. We said nothing more for a while, until the line was clearly trees, some five miles off. Then the leading ox raised his head and mooed. I feared he was about to die, but it was because he smelled water. We had conquered the desert.

A LITTER PROBLEM?

The gold rush wagons left an amazing amount of "litter" on their journey westward. One forty-niner, having seen the tools, equipment, even food left at the roadside, said: "If I were going again, I'd start with a light wagon and some mules, and gather up the rest along the road." Fort Laramie was called "Cape Sacrifice" because of the amount dumped on the Plains nearby. (Traders would not buy from the travelers the things they could go out and pick up on the Plains later.) Almost anything could be found on the trail. One man found countless tools, cooking stoves, food, a carved bookcase, and an iron safe!

But the deserts claimed the most. In 1850, almost 2,000 wagons were left there. Not just wagons — one 1850 group found the trail so choked with dead and dying cattle that they had to make a new trail around them. A man called Calvin Taylor, crossing in 1850, said that the stink and the look of the desert reminded him of a battlefield. In 1850 one man tried to count all he passed. It came to: 2,381 horses and mules, 433 oxen, and 787 wagons with goods worth some $100,000 in the Carson Desert alone. Others at the time made the value closer to a million dollars.

CHAPTER 5

Mountain Crossing

The Relief Company, shown here guiding wagons through the mountains, was set up after demands in the newspapers that the tragedy that struck the Donner Party (see box on page 23) in 1846–1847 not happen again. Money was collected from local citizens in areas along the trail (like California and Nevada). As the numbers crossing the mountains grew, so the local charities found it hard to cope. The government was urged to take over the job. In November 1849, California began to organize relief with government money.

But we had yet to cross the mountains. There was some talk of leaving the wagon, for the sake of speed, but all we had in the world was on it, and there were not enough animals to carry us all in safety. So, on the morning of October 12, we set out, and it was heavy going, for the road by the river was sandy, and our wheels sank in deeply. It looked to be slow going. We saw dust ahead of us but took it to be another late party, who we would never catch up with. But it became clear that the dust was coming toward us. Indians? When they came nearer, we saw it was two horsemen, each of them leading a fine mule. As they came up to us, they smiled and asked who we were. They told us they were from the Relief Company set up by the government to help late emigrants over the mountains. They had met with the party we had passed and been told about us, so had come to find us. Our new friends then guided us to a spot where we could rest for the rest of the day and said they would help us pack up all that we could from the wagon. That which could not be packed, we would have to leave. They said there had been two days of snow at the top of the Sierras; they had only just gotten through. But then the weather had cleared. If we made haste, leaving the wagon, which would not fit through the passes, we might get through before the passes were blocked for winter.

Everything was arranged for an early morning start, and I felt there was much to be grateful for. At first I found the mule quite difficult to ride, but I soon got used to it. Our friends set off ahead, for they were due back, leaving us clear instructions as to the way. On October 17, we reached the head of the Carson Valley. We had been joined by a small company of men. The road became very rough, steep, and difficult; it was hard work for the men to drive the mules on. The canyon we were passing through got narrower and narrower, hundreds of feet above us. At times it seemed almost to meet above our heads, which gave us far less light to travel by. It got harder to keep the animals on the right trail, which was hard to follow. We came to a creek, which seemed to have a good crossing point and a better trail on the far side than ours, yet we had been told to stick to the canyon. While we were trying to decide which way to go, one of the mules, the one carrying nearly all of the party's food, rushed off up the trail in the canyon. My husband chased after it, the cattle, who were unsettled, crowded in on us, and Mary fell into the creek. She was unhurt, but while I was getting her out, the cattle scattered. When the animals were all together again, there was an argument as to which way to go, and one of the men who had joined us, DeLou, insisted on following the steep trail up the canyon. So we went on, but the way soon became almost impassable, and the cattle could not manage. It grew dark, and Mary was fretful. We were lost, and I had no idea where my husband was. Then we heard a gun fired and made our way to the sound. With much scrambling, we found our way back to the creek bed and, in less than an hour, found my husband and the rest at a camping place.

The next day, we climbed the first of the two ridges at the top of the mountains. The way was so steep that we could do nothing but hold on and let the mules find their own way. That night, when we made camp, there was snow in a ravine close by, and the water froze in our pans, which were quite close to the fire. But the morning was bright and sunny and toward noon, being ahead of the others, I came out on a rocky height where I found I was looking DOWN, down into the Sacramento Valley. We made our way down. It got less cold but more dusty. On the night of October 21, we were awakened by cries and shots from the men's camp, which was a short way off from ours. Some Indians had fired arrows into the camp, and one man was wounded, but not seriously. On the evening of October 24, we reached a place described in our guide as "Pleasant Valley Gold Mines," where we found several tents and a few men at work with their gold pans. The miners said that these mines were almost worked out, but that a new settlement, called Weaverville, nearby, was growing into a town. We decided to go there.

THE DONNER PARTY

The Donner Party headed for California in 1846. They were late in the season, like Sarah Royce, so they and some others took a shortcut. When they rejoined the main trail at Humbolt's River, they found that those who had gone the long way were now ahead. The Donner Party saw they needed help, so sent two men on to Sutter's Fort, on the other side of the mountains. The men who went on arrived too late. Rescuers with food and mules went into the mountains, but the way was blocked with snow. They hung food in the trees, in case anyone got through, and went back.

In mid-January, two men and five women from the Donner Party came down from the mountains. They said the rest were at a place called Donner Lake. Fifteen people had set off to ask for help and show relief people the way back. Only these seven had made it. The people at the lake were sick and starving. The seven who had just arrived had been forced to eat their dead companions to survive long enough to get down. A relief group left at once; three more followed. All took food and brought as many people back as they could. Forty-two of the party died. Forty-seven lived. Without the relief men, there would have been just seven survivors.

CHAPTER 6

Weaverville

Weaverville was a camp of tents, many of them very irregularly placed. In one part, following the line of the ravine, there was already quite a row of them, all a considerable distance apart. We added ourselves to that row and began to make ourselves at home. Soon the mountains above us were blocked with snow. Only one more party after us made it through the mountains this year.

And now began my first experience of a California mining camp. The sense of safety that came from being safe from Indians, or death in the desert or the snows, was restful and, like a child playing house, I sang as I arranged our few comforts in our tent. Still, there was a lurking sense of insecurity. There was only a cloth wall between us and the out-of-doors. I was told the sad story of how three thieves in a nearby town had been tried and hanged by a committee of residents — this gave the town the name of Hangtown. We were assured that everyone in Weaverville was honest, not likely to steal, but yet we could so easily be walked in on. I soon found I had no reason to fear. While I was sitting and sewing in my tent, I heard men cutting wood on the hill behind. Presently one man called out, "Take care the way the wood rolls. There's a woman and child in that tent; don't frighten them."

The miners all seemed very pleasant, bidding good-day if we met with them. One man stopped and asked if he could speak with Mary, saying there were so few women and children there as yet, and that Mary reminded him of his youngest sister at home. It turned out that he was a doctor who had come to seek gold to better support his widowed mother and family. It turned out that many of the miners, despite dressing in mining clothes and working with a pick and shovel, were gentlemen. There were lawyers, scientists, and merchants, as well as mechanics and farmers. In almost every mining town, there were enough people who wanted order, control, or very much influence, the less orderly spirits. These facts soon became apparent to me, and before long I felt as secure in my tent with the curtain tied in front, as I had in my house in town with locked and bolted doors.

There were, as in every group of people, those who were more rowdy and lawless, less gentle and kind. But even they, mostly, knew it was safer to let law and order rule. All of them, except for a few desperate exceptions, were willing to let the lovers of order enjoy their rights and order the towns. As long as they were not expected to work at creating order themselves, they were prepared to accept it. As for the desperate exceptions, they were, at least in the places that we lived, so overawed by the severe punishments that others (like the thieves in Hangtown) suffered, that they dared not act on their inclinations. In those early days, life and property were safe in the mines.

When I say that life and property were safe, I do not mean that you could act without forethought. If you were foolish enough to associate with desperadoes and gamblers then, of course, you constantly risked your money and your life. But, it has to be said, that is true of any place, be it Weaverville, Philadelphia, or London.

We lived in Weaverville for two months, and in all that time I had only a few brief glimpses of the objectionable side of life in these towns. Indeed, I ought not even to say "glimpses," for my experiences were, almost totally, a matter of being told about things, not experiencing them myself. There was, on the opposite side of the ravine, a very large tent, or rather two tents cobbled together, which, at first, I took to be a boardinghouse. Then I realized that it was, in fact, a drinking and gambling saloon. We often heard a lot of noise coming from there, but only once did anything out of the way happen. Past midnight, one dark, rainy night, we were startled from sleep by a loud shout, followed by several running footsteps and three or four pistol shots. We looked out. The only light in the town came from the saloon, but there was no more noise. The next morning, we were told by a person who had gone to investigate that a gambler who had lost many times and was set to lose again had snatched all the money from the center of the table in a sudden movement and fled before he could be stopped. The shots had been fired after him, but he had escaped in the darkness.

The need for law and order was the same all over the West. There were too many lawbreakers and too few law enforcers to go around. Many towns, in desperation, set up groups, called vigilante groups, that caught and punished criminals. Vigilante punishment seemed to consist mainly of hanging. This vigilante hanging was photographed (by more than one photographer at a time!) in Kansas in 1894. The photographs were displayed as a warning.

The Mines of Placerville, *painted by Albertus Browere in 1855. Placerville was the first big camp after the 1848–1849 discoveries of gold in California. It was first named Dry Diggings, then called Hangtown (this is the place Sarah Royce was told about when she arrived in Weaverville). In 1851 the name was changed again. The settlement was called Placerville, after the amount of "**placer**" gold (gold near the surface) in the area. When the placer gold was all dug, miners had to resort to digging deep mines. This was more often done by companies than by small groups of men.*

There are three methods of mining shown in the picture:
digging *the ore up with a pickax*
*"**panning**" (washing small amounts of dirt in the river)*
*"**cradle washing**," a mechanized, more efficient, sort of panning.*

My other glimpses of the less-refined side of the town were through a woman, the only other woman in the town. There had been a third woman when we arrived in the town, a lovely woman but in very delicate health. We had known her in that first large company we rode with, the company we crossed the Platte with, for she had ridden on horseback for her health and would sometimes ride alongside our wagon and talk to me. But the invalid lady and her husband did not stay long in Weaverville. When the rains came, they moved farther south, hoping to find weather more suited to her well-being.

The woman who remained was a plain person, who had come from one of the western states with her husband and had only ever lived in the country before. We had already had some conversation, as we went about our duties; we would talk as we cooked over the campfires. I had not seen her for some time, however, when she called in on me in a very happy mood. She told me that the man who kept the boardinghouse had offered her the grand sum of $100 a month to cook for his boarders, for they complained greatly about his cooking. He was even prepared to let her have someone to do the washing up, if she would just do the cooking.

She had been doing the job for some days when she called on me. It was clear that she was very full of the fact that she was earning a wage. She said that her husband was also very glad that his wife could earn so much money for a chore that she was well able to do at little inconvenience to him.

Again I saw little of her for some time, no doubt her work left little enough time for her own chores, let alone socializing. Then, again, she called. This time she was very much changed in style. She had been plain to look at and plainly dressed, nothing out-of-the-way about her at all. Now her hair was done in a youthful style, her clothes trimmed with ribbons and such, and her manner of speaking very affected and condescending. She came to tell me that there was to be a "ball" at the saloon in a few days. Several ladies, all of whom lived in different camps close by and several from Hangtown, were coming. She came to say that I could go if I wanted, that I would be very welcome. I laughingly declined, saying I was no dancer, nor had I suitable clothes for such an occasion. I think the meeting happened as expected, but I did not get even a glimpse of its glories, it being in the saloon on the other side of the ravine. This woman left the town soon after, and I never saw her again.

Soon after we arrived in Weaverville, my husband also met a traveling acquaintance from early in our journey. This man had **washed out** a little gold and was eager to go into business. He and some other men were sure that this new mining settlement needed a store, but they did not have the experience to start one. He then remembered my husband saying that he had been in trade and hoped to be so here, and they offered him a share in the store. They proposed that they would build a store while he went to Sacramento City for goods to stock it.

So the building began. The plan was to cut wood for the frame and split **shakes** for the roof and sides. But it was not easy to get men to help them; all were so absorbed in washing out gold or hunting for some to wash, that they could not think of anything else. On all sides the **gold pans** were rattling, the **cradles** rocking, and the water splashing. The best that they could manage was to cut some strong tent poles and ridges and to set up two good-sized tents, one behind the other. The back one was to live in; the front was the store. We were offered a large cookstove, which we placed at the junction of the two tents. We curtained off part of the back tent for me, leaving a space around the cookstove for dining and cooking. One man was to sleep in the store, we were to sleep in the back, and the other two had a small tent at the side. They managed to find some packing boxes to make a rough counter and shelves, and we were set.

WOMEN IN THE MINING TOWNS

The mining towns of California, especially in the first years after 1849, had very few women living there. Sometimes there was only one woman in an entire town. The miners reacted to these women in several different ways. There were some miners who were irritated by a woman living in the town or camp, feeling that they were expected to behave better if there was a woman around. Others welcomed women, partly because they reminded them of "home" and also because they took time to make things more homelike around them. Women were more likely to be involved in running stores and boardinghouses than they were to be looking for gold.

FOOD

Most miners had a very boring diet. They ate stewed dried beans and bread or hard, dry "biscuit" made from flour and water. They drank coffee or whiskey. Dried meat was a luxury; even more so, in the early years, were fresh vegetables and fruit. They ate better as the years went on and as people came to farm California — more fresh food was available. But not between 1849–1852. Because what the food miners usually ate was so bad, food like Sarah Royce's fresh beef would have been in great demand. Other women found that skills that were seen as quite ordinary at home, like cooking, were in great demand in the mining towns. Cooking was a common skill back East — not so in the mines. The $100 offered by the boardinghouse keeper to a woman to cook for his lodgers (see page 26) was not unusual (women were also offered this amount to do laundry work). The average wage for this sort of work back East would have been closer to $10 a month. Some women preferred to work from their homes. One woman in the mining towns in 1850 baked a batch of apple pies (made with dried apple) each morning, which she sold for $1 each. She always had more customers than pies.

Prices for other goods are discussed in the box on page 31.

We were soon settled in our new quarters, the goods arrived from Sacramento, and business was opened. As one of the partners had been in the meat business before, we bought cattle to fatten and sold beef, as well as everything else. This drew quite a crowd every morning, for fresh meat was not yet plentiful in the mining towns. Not all of the men devoted all of their time to the store. Two of them continued mining; so, when there were a lot of people in the store, I helped to serve them. This meant I got acquainted with most of the inhabitants of Weaverville. Most of them were men. Most of them were used to living in an orderly community and tried to impose that same order on our town. They were men of religion and morality, yet they had come a long way from their old lives, had had a hard journey, and had long been separated from the old home comforts. Yet they tried to keep their old customs as best they could, especially in my presence, for women were, as yet, unusual in mining towns.

There were some men who were definitely of a different class. They were rough-reared frontiersmen, almost as ignorant of civilized life as if they were savages. They were more reckless and wild, even in the face of the restraints of "official" town policy. Yet they could not show what they had never known. And while they did not know how to be civilized, they certainly were never rude, threatening, or impertinent toward me, even if their manners were a little rough and ready. Both sorts of men came for meat and other provisions in the early morning. We even had some Indians as customers, for the Indians, too, were washing out gold in the nearby ravines. The varied customers kept the two or three of us very busy; the men had certainly been right about the need for a store. We were paid almost exclusively in gold dust. It took longer to weigh that than it would have done to take coins and give change. But coins were very rare in the mines in the early days, so we had our gold scale and weights, and I soon became very expert in handling them.

It was a while after we had been there that I noticed that, among all the bustle of the town, the working and eating, buying and selling, there was an undertone of sadness and discontent. These men had come to California to become easily and rapidly rich. They had endured great hardships to reach the goldfields, only to find that they had to work very hard to find gold at all. Even if they found it, they had to wash it out, and then they had to use it to buy the necessities of living, which cost more than at home because of the trouble of getting it there. Some of them even called it a "God-forsaken" place; certainly there were many complaints that they were fools to have left home. At home they had had more comfort for certain. Most of them had had good jobs and homes but had given up a steady wage in the hopes of finding more money quickly.

Nor did most of them give up mining, for the folly had a hold on them. They thought that the next day would be the "big day" kept them pressing on. Every few days we heard of new discoveries, farther afield. These were, more often than not, announced by chronic prospectors who kept the whole community in a ferment of expectation. They seldom came to anything but kept many of the men from settling to anything, even to a particular plot on the goldfields.

The sense of discontent was not just related to the lack of quick riches. The conditions that the men lived in were so bad as to be unhealthy. They arrived in bad health anyway, worn out with the traveling, often sick from eating the bad food, which was all they had. There were tales of men who had come the whole way without once having taken off their clothes, even their boots, to wash; who had lived on salted meat and biscuit the whole time. This poor diet and poor hygiene was bound to encourage disease. Even ignoring such extreme cases, it was true that overexertion, changes in lifestyle, and depression led to a lot of sickness. Many people fell sick in our neighborhood, and some died, despite kind efforts to save them.

Miners in a store, having their gold weighed. As late as the 1890s (when this picture was taken) miners were still paying for their goods with gold dust instead of money. The store seems to have been run as a café as well; the young boy in the middle is holding some cups and plates. The store must have been doing well, because the storekeeper has been able to buy a lot of stock.

CHAPTER 7

Sacramento

My husband came home from a trip to Sacramento with a severe attack of cholera. For some days he could do nothing, not even work in the store. Just as he was getting better, I was laid low by a slow but powerful fever. As soon as I could be moved, it was decided to move on, for sickness was so common in that place that we felt in need of a change. As soon as I could be moved, a wagon was found, and I was bedded down in that. A seat was made for Mary near to me, and our things were loaded. On December 27, we set out for Sacramento City.

By now it was nearly midwinter, but as we moved west from the south fork of American River, it seemed to turn toward spring very rapidly. Grass sprang up, flowers bloomed, and birds sang. The milder weather, bright sun, and pleasant landscape did much to help me feel better. I began to get my appetite back. On the second evening of our journey, we camped near a house where a lady rented rooms and cooked and washed for travelers. I was so much better that I asked her if she could bake a **sweet potato** for me, a crop that had recently been grown in the area and sold in the mines. She had one, so she did so. She charged me 75 cents for it, but as we were not having to pay for accommodation — nowhere being more comfortable than the wagon — we paid the price of the sweet potato. I have to say, though, that we thought it the most expensive we had encountered, even against the prices in the mines.

A picture of Sacramento in 1850. It is drawn from the bottom of J Street and shows I, J, and K streets. Notice the trees being cleared to build new houses, the tent houses of new arrivals, and the more solid wooden houses, warehouses, and stores by the waterfront.

I have not really talked about prices, as they have been written about so much already. But the mining towns were expensive — fresh meat was half a dollar a pound, butter a dollar, and all other things proportionally expensive. Yet we found when we got to Sacramento City that things were even more expensive here, if you were buying as a single customer, not as a storekeeper. One of our number was charged a dollar for a single onion; another paid twenty-five cents for four pints of milk — and that we saw the man water down. But that is to go on ahead.

On January 1, 1850, we arrived at Sutter's Fort. I used to read of it as a girl, saying that one day I would go there, would gaze on the Pacific Ocean, yet little thought I would actually be able to do so. We took our noon break there and placed the wagon so that I could sit up and look at the old buildings surrounded by a wide wall. Now things were more civilized; the wide gates, so often shut against Indians in my girlhood stories, were wide open. We rode on, and, before evening had fallen, reached Sacramento City. The city was a strange one. There were more tents and cloth houses to be seen than any other kind of dwelling. It was not that strange to see people making a home of their wagon, so we did that for a day or two, until we could get enough wood to lay a good floor, over which we stretched a well-made tent. We put our cookstove in here and now were home, though I was not yet well enough to sit up all day.

We intended to build a house here, as soon as we could. My husband had bought the land, intending to build a general grocery business, even before I was taken sick. But just as we arrived, the skies, which had been clear for several weeks, clouded over. It began to rain the day we put up our tent, and the great rainy season set in. Day after day it rained, with only very short intervals of sunshine. Then it would cloud over and rain, rain, rain would pour down for hours. Two of my husband's partners in the Weaverville business had joined with him in this venture. They were impatient to build and open business, but nothing could be done in this weather but care for the cattle. As they came to and fro, I listened from my curtained off corner to all the gossip they brought of places and people that I did not yet know but grew impatient to meet. After a few days, the topic of conversation became more ominous. The rivers — both the Sacramento and the American rivers — were rising; especially the American, whose banks were very low just behind the city and were threatening to overflow. Old settlers were talking of the times it had burst its banks and the "sloo" — mud and water — had spread through the city. No one could agree if there was any real danger, but most seemed to think that if it did burst, the "sloo" would drain straight into the Sacramento River, passing the town by with little damage.

STORES AND PRICES

Miners were shocked by prices in mining town stores. But it is hardly surprising that food was expensive, with the difficulties of getting food and the high price charged for the food in the first place (food for the mining towns was bought in the bigger towns, like Sacramento). In 1850 a miner would be lucky to average an ounce of gold dust a day. This was worth about $15. Prices of food in mining areas averaged out at about:

tea and coffee	$1 a lb.
sugar	$2 a lb.
bread (one loaf)	$1
milk (four pints)	$0.50
eggs (10)	$5
tobacco	$2 a lb.
whiskey (bottle)	$5
molasses (a pint)	$0.50
dried beef	$2 a lb.
flour	$11 a lb.

These are only rough estimates. Some traders charged less. There were many storekeepers who charged more.

In the 1850s, people also took food and water over the mountains to sell to those crossing from Salt Lake City to California. They could charge very high prices. Some of them even set up tent stands in the desert! Here, water cost up to $1 for eight pints. Some of the people who ran these stands were happy just to make a profit and help travelers. Others charged such high prices that they were known as "land pirates."

CHAPTER 8

Flooded Out!

On the evening of January 9, one of our friends arrived, crying, "The water's coming!" We hoped it was a false alarm, but it was not. Among the houses nearby was one belonging to a doctor, which was not finished yet but was enclosed and roofed, with an upper floor. Our friend ran to ask for permission to use the upper floor; my husband was to get Mary and myself ready for a fast removal. He worked as rapidly as he could, gathering up bedding and clothes in a big bundle, with things that needed to stay most dry in the middle. By the time our friend returned with permission, we were almost packed up.

The water level was rising fast, but we made it to the house safely, with only our shoes getting wet. Sitting on the upper floor, I could hear the water rippling and gurgling down the street and spilling in over the sill of the lower floor. It was evidently rising very fast. The men, ferrying things between the tent and the house, soon found the water so high that they had to abandon the rest of our things to the flood. Now more people arrived to shelter in the house. We curtained off an area for ourselves. Most of the men gathered around a stove that the workmen had left there. The house filled and filled, with men, women, and children. We heard the next day that, by midnight, there were some fifty people in the rest of the house. As soon as we felt safe from the dangers, we began to worry about those who were still in danger. It became clear, from the crossing of boats and the calling of men, that there were many people out and about giving what assistance they could. So far, all those who had been in danger had been rescued. Hundreds of people had flocked and were flocking to the high ground well above the water, some two miles to the east of where we were, and all were somehow being provided for.

In the morning, we heard more boats. They came close to the house, and we found that most of the other people were being taken away, either to go to San Francisco, or to the high ground I spoke of. All in our end but for our little party went, too. As soon as I could, I got up, dressed, and looked out of the window. For miles north and south I could see nothing but water, covered with boats, rafts, even some kind of canoes. Our friends set off with others for the ridge, where much of the provisions of the town had been taken to prevent famine. Soon they returned with enough to live on for a few days. Luckily we had enough wood for the stove, too. Our friends also arranged that boats would check on us from time to time, especially if the water level rose, to make sure all was well. We began to talk about what to do and wondered if it might not be best to take the next steamer to San Francisco. Other boats were making the journey but were too loaded to be safe. We were better as we were than if we made for the ridge. So for several days, we were imprisoned by the waters.

Sacramento, being between two rivers, was often flooded. This photograph shows the flood of 1862. This is K Street, the street on the far right of the picture on page 30, where the trees are being cleared. Notice how the town has grown since 1850. There has been a lot of building. The town now has, from looking at the signs, two public bathhouses on this street alone!

CHAPTER 9

San Francisco

NATURAL DISASTERS

Sarah Royce was always aware of the weather, both during the journey and while living in the mining towns. Neither the wagon nor the tent homes that she lived in gave much shelter from bad weather, especially from storms with both wind and rain.

Sacramento, sited as it was, often flooded. It is hard to see why it grew up where it did, except that it was far enough from the mountains to be on fairly level ground and near a river that led to the ocean, for shipping. Sacramento was not the only place to suffer natural disasters. San Francisco suffered occasional earthquakes. The most severe of these often started fires when wooden houses, which frequently had wood-fired stoves, fell in on themselves.

News that came from the ridge was not good. People fell sick, there was little shelter, and many had nothing but the clothes they stood in. Still, we were not totally safe either. One night there was a strong wind that grew to a heavy gale. It whipped up the waters around the house, which was, you will remember, a very ordinary, unfinished, frame house. The waves crashed against the sides of the house so that it rocked and shook until we seemed in danger of capsizing. It was impossible to sleep. I tried to plan what to do if the house should go. But we were in luck. The house did not go, and the next day news came that the old steamer *McKim* was in port taking on passengers for San Francisco.

On the morning of January 15, a boat came to take us to the steamer. As we made our way there, we passed through an area with more houses, so in the end we were going down the middle of a street with houses on either side. They were all submerged to at least half the height of the ground floor. When we reached the steamer, we were helped on board, and it set off. The journey was long, slow, and dreary. There was mile after mile of muddy water, with the odd hill rising out of it, on which were clustered groups of people, mostly men, and cattle huddling together. We anchored in the Bay of San Francisco on the morning of the following day. Telegraph Hill was directly in front of us. We were not allowed too close to the shore, so we were ferried off the steamer by smaller boats. It was nearly noon when we landed on the wharves. I was allowed to sit in a warehouse office while my husband went to look for rooms. He returned to say there were none at all, but that we could eat in The Montgomery House, a saloon nearby, where Mary and I could wait while he tried again.

As we entered, we were told to go into a room that had no floorcovering, one table, and a few chairs. There was a cloth partition between this "sitting room" and the "dining room," which was furnished in pretty much the same way. The barroom was across the passage and was the only room in the whole place with a stove, apart from the kitchen. We waited while the men searched. There were no rooms to be found, so we were glad when the landlord offered us rooms. The stairs led up to a passage that ran the length of the building. The rooms were spaces some 2.5 feet wide and 6 feet long, partitioned off by cloth sheets. The landlord proposed that we take the two rooms at the far end, this being the most private space that could be had, so we did. The next day our search for lodgings began again, with the same result. Then came the rain, and our situation became worse, for everyone in our hotel had to stay indoors, either in their small space or in the comfortless rooms below. I was driven to seek out the stove in the barroom, with some trepidation, and found that the men there cheerfully made room for me and Mary.

Things could have been far worse. Everyone did their best to get along; there was no drunkenness or selfish behavior. But we could not live this way for long. Then, on Saturday morning, one of our friends arrived with the **pastor** of the recently established Protestant Church of San Francisco. He said that a friend of his had just built a house to split into **tenements**. Only one was finished, that of his family, but another was soon to be ready if we would like to rent it. There was at least one room finished, which we could go to at once. We quickly accepted and, before night fell, were moved into the room he spoke of. It seemed a great luxury to us. I was also now able to go to church, and this made me very happy. I realized how long it had been since I had been able to worship God with fellow Christians, and I was glad of the chance to do so now.

I now began to get around more. At first, just a short journey tired me, but I got healthier and healthier and took Mary for longer and longer walks to explore the city. We found places that had a good view of the Bay and the variety of stores and houses that the city had to show. Two months later, we were able to move into our tenement, which, though mostly a paper and cloth construction, had been well constructed and furnished. Here we found we were surrounded by many like us, churchgoing people with whom we could socialize easily, and from whom we learned a lot about the City; some had been there a while.

A picture of San Francisco in 1851. It is more built-up than Sacramento (see picture on page 30) and seems to have grown up in a more random way — there are no obvious great lines of streets. Most of the buildings are wooden, and quite a few have more than one story. Notice the mix of people. There are people who look like miners and people who look more like tradesmen. There are women and children. There are also several Chinese people. These people may be from the settlement that later grew into the famous Chinatown. Sarah Royce found this area of the town once she was able to get out and explore (see page 36).

Much has been said of the dark side of San Francisco at this time. But any newcomer in the city could seek and find good people to be with. The city did draw to itself people from all over, many of whom hoped to get gold as quickly as possible. Many of them intended to get it by hard work, but there were those who wished to get it with as little work as possible, who had few scruples as to how they did this. The city was home to all sorts of people, from many walks of life. And not just different classes, different nations, too. While we were walking one day, Mary and I came upon a number of odd-looking tents, many selling strange-looking bundles, boxes, and toys. It took me but a minute to see that these people were Chinese. It was an unexpected sight, this little beginning of what was to become the famous Chinatown, and I was, at first, as entranced as Mary. Then I began to feel out-of-place so turned to find a way out. I was stopped by an elderly Chinaman, carrying a blue cloth sack. He said a word or two in broken English, stooped down, shook hands with Mary, and gave her a toy.

As time passed, we saw the beginning of the system of **street grading**, the fire of May 4, 1850, the onset of cholera, and California's joining the United States. The city was a place of many comings and goings, much buying and selling, and a lot of speculations in investments. Many people embarked on business schemes that were so badly thought through that they were doomed to fail; certainly more failed than succeeded.

For nearly three years after our first arrival in San Francisco, we lived on the borders of the Bay. While here I noticed an example of the effects of the Californian emigration on domestic life that made me thankful that we had survived as we had. A man we had known on the Plains, who had spoken much about his wife and family whom he was to return to was told that his wife was seeking to divorce him, for she thought he had abandoned her. He seemed upset but did nothing to remedy the matter and was soon behaving like a single man. Certainly life in California was hard; it did put strain on relationships. This was true both when it caused separation and estrangement, as in this man's case, and when it caused a falling out between those who had arrived together. One or other of the couple felt themselves hard-done-by by the change and fell to blaming the other. Certainly women felt the isolation most, for there were few of us in California at the time and so, except in the cities, there were seldom other women to talk to and mix with. This scarcity of women had another bad effect. There were few women for the single men to court, so they would compete, sometimes even fight, for the attention of women, single or, if there were no other, married. This led many a woman who would have been settled in the East to leave her husband in the hopes of doing better in a second, even third, marriage.

But I will now talk of our home on the Bay. We spent only a short while in the city of San Francisco itself, for we did not find city life pleasing. Our home on the Bay was close enough to the city for us to get supplies easily, yet far enough away for us not to have the nuisance of living all packed in together, as we had been. Here we spent our second spring in California, the first having been spent in San Francisco. Here on the Bay, the changes in the seasons were more noticeable. San Francisco was often affected by strong winds and fogs, at all times of year, which made it less pleasant to live in. Here every smoothly rolling hill was covered in blossom; the flat land of the valley was like a gorgeous carpet rolling from our bayside village back to the mountains. The air was full of birdsong.

The children really enjoyed life in the village. Mary ran around picking flowers and making playhouses. The baby, for we now had a second child, sat in her cradle or her little chair laughing, watching her sister. My children were both happy and healthy. I had regained my health entirely. Life with my family could never be dull or lonely. My one regret was that our village had not, as yet, a church to call its own. But there was a schoolhouse, and church meetings, led by a visiting minister, were held every other Sunday. The ministers showed a lot of interest in the Sunday school that we ran weekly, which was run to suit all varieties of Christian worship.

The Chinese community in San Francisco was a large one, but there were Chinese people all over California. Some of them joined mining communities, like these Chinese miners photographed at the head of the Auburn Ravine in 1852. The Chinese people here seem to be working alongside the Americans. Things did not always go this well (see box on page 36). Americans were hostile to other races, too. The Americans let the Mexicans and Chinese move in if they had a useful skill — laundry work, cooking, even mining skills — but they did not think that anyone but Americans should benefit from American gold.

The miners here are "washing out" chunks of earth, looking for "placer" gold.

So we found life in this village on the Bay far more to our liking than we had found living in the city. As the seasons passed, the colors changed. The rich green on the hills became flecked with faded spots. These spots gradually spread until nearly the whole surface was a rich old gold. And when the wind came, the trees seemed to laugh and dance, even the stately evergreen oaks. The wildflowers changed with the seasons, adding different splashes of color to the fields, through which the cattle constantly moved, grazing and calling, adding life to the scene. I felt as if I would never get tired of watching these changes.

Yet for all I felt things to be quite "poetic" in their beauty, there was menace, even here. One hot August afternoon, when I was, as usual, alone with the children, as I passed across our kitchen/dining room doorway, I saw, near the front door, an object on the ground just outside. It was moving along quite slowly, always coming toward the house.

I went to investigate and saw it was a creature that covered a space that looked to me like the size of an eight-year-old boy's hand. In the center was a round, hairy body that had a projecting, hairy head. Legs, looking like slender, hairy fingers, with the knuckles set well in, strode on each side of it. It was getting quicker, still moving toward the house. I had never seen one before, but I had read about them and knew what it was in an instant. It was a **tarantula**! I was terrified that it would get underneath the house. If it did so, I would never find it, never know where it might be. It might manage to crawl up through some opening or other into the house, the very thought of which made my blood run cold. It could go anywhere.

Temporary homes were made out of all sorts of materials. Sarah Royce and her family lived for much of the time in what was, in effect, a wooden-framed tent. Other people, in more densely wooded areas, made their homes from whole logs. The woman in this picture is standing outside a bark house. The strips of bark were hammered onto a wooden frame, with wooden beams across the roof to keep it on. The rest of the wood was used for firewood and other sorts of building. At the back of the house, on the left of the picture, standing on two branches to let the air flow under it, is the woodbox for her fuel. The almost separate triangular part of the building (next to the woodbox) is obviously supposed to have a particular purpose — the house next door has a piece like it, too. Perhaps it was the cooking area, separate and easily pulled away from the rest of the house if it caught fire.

I stood, for an instant, as if turned to stone. It might get into Mary's low bed, even into the baby's cradle. It might go to where the children were playing, near the house. These thoughts all came to me in an instant, and at the same time I found myself springing through the door and grabbing a huge piece of wood. I dashed to where it was, so as to be directly in its path, and dropped the piece of wood on it. I had literally crushed the enemy but found I was shaking all over from the encounter.

I at once searched the house to see if there were any other creatures lurking around the house. This seemed a sensible enough move, but I was then forced to stop myself from a constant searching, which was far from rational. However, this was my only encounter with one of these creatures. A friend of mine, who knew about such things, said it was unusual for them to be seen except in undisturbed places, that you usually had to hunt for them. He also said it was an unusually large specimen, and I got credit for having taken on a really formidable foe.

The seasons rolled on, and we reached another spring. Time seemed to move slowly and peacefully, with few events like the one I have described above to disrupt its natural progression from one season to another. We gloried in this one just as much as the one before; familiarity had not dimmed our wonder. Living here seemed to give me my childhood back again. I look back on that time and see the colors as clearer, brighter than ordinary colors, and I seem to remember that it was a time when we were almost constantly laughing. I am glad that my girls, especially Mary, who had had to endure the rigors of the journey west, had this magic, peaceful time in their lives.

However, it was time to be moving on. My husband and I talked about this for a long time. He wanted to open a store in a mining town again. So it was decided that we would journey once more into the interior of the state. We were to head back toward the mountains to live in a mining town. This town was close by the mountains but not actually in them. It was beside a river, some twenty miles from Sacramento City, and we had been assured that it was in a healthy place and did not have a lot of sickness among the people who lived there.

We gathered our things together and, in the fall of our second year in the village, we set off away from it. I was sad to go, as was Mary, but the baby was quite content as long as she was with her family, in the way that Mary had been quite content to leave our home in the East and make the journey west.

NATURAL DANGERS

Sarah Royce and her family chose to live away from the city, so that they did not have to be cramped, and so they could avoid the noise and bustle. Cities were also supposed to be more dangerous. In cities people were more at risk from other people. In more rural surroundings, there was a risk from the creatures that had lived in the area long before people moved in.

Besides tarantulas there were scorpions, which had a deadly sting. There were not really many greater dangers. But even domestic animals could be problematic, if not dangerous. Few animals stampeded as Sarah Royce's cattle had on the journey west, but if they came too close to a frame house, they could damage it without even meaning to. One settler woke early in the morning to hear her cattle scratching themselves on the wall of her frame tent house. Seconds later, the house fell in on top of her! Luckily, she says, the stove had gone out.

CHAPTER 10

Moving On

So once again, we were in a mining town. The sands of the riverbed were said to be rich in gold, which could only be washed out while the bed was dry, in the summer. But gold had also been found in the bluffs on the north side of the stream. A large amount of water was needed to wash this out, which the river would supply. Some San Francisco gentlemen had organized themselves into a company which, they said, would ensure a good water supply. They planned to dam the river some distance above the **bar**, raise the water level (using a steam engine) to the required height, run it through a large **flume** at the back of the diggings, far enough back to give them a good fall. They would then sell the water to the miners by the square inch, distributing it by means of small flumes to the place it was required. It seemed very complicated, but they were confident of success.

The necessary buildings were erected, the steam engine was constructed, the great flume was built — all at great expense. While this was being done, a group of miners, among them a few families, gathered at the site. Tents and cloth houses were put up, sometimes a **shanty** of bits of log and board. We chose a very pretty spot on the bluff, shaded by some young oak trees and surrounded by shrubs that formed a natural hedge. Our house was of cloth, but it had an excellent frame, which was proved a few weeks after we moved in, when one of the longest and most terrific gales I have ever experienced hit our town, accompanied by heavy rain. For three days and nights the floods fell, and the wind beat, and while our frame bent and moved, it did not fall. There were, it is true, two or three leaks, but they were minor, and the outcome that I most feared — that the children would catch colds — did not occur.

Our house was not large, but I worked hard to make it comfortable. I covered the floor entirely, partly with dark matting and partly with carpet. I curtained off one end for a bedroom and, by having a trundle bed for the two oldest children — I now had three — I managed to make room for hanging clothes and storing trunks. The rest of the house was divided, more by the arrangement of furniture than by actual partitions, into a kitchen, dining room, and parlor. The kitchen consisted of the cookstove, the woodbox, and a cupboard that I had made with my own hands from a dry goods box. The dining room consisted of a table and a couple of chairs. It is true that I had to use my dining table to prepare bread, pie, and cakes on baking days, but at least I did not have far to go to put them in the oven! The parlor was my pride. There was a small table with a cloth against the wall, a few knickknacks, and a few books. There was a narrow shelf above it, with yet more books and what paper we had. There were two or three **plush** covered seats that Mary and I called "ottomans."

The frames of these seats were rough boxes, which I stuffed and covered myself. There was also a rocking chair, but the pride of it all was my **melodeon**. It was said to be the first in California and had been used in a church in Sacramento till it came to be mine. There was little time for music in the day (except on Sundays), but at night, when the children were in bed, and the store — for we were running the store in this town — kept my husband away, I would play for myself, and the bare rafters and cloth walls became a cathedral to me.

But we did not stay here long, for the Water Company was one of those San Francisco business ventures that I spoke of that had not been thought through. The expenses of setting up and running the company meant that the charge to the miners had to be set so high that they could not afford to pay for it. The miners and the company men met. The company men showed how, to make ends meet, they had to charge the high prices that they did. The miners showed how, to make ends meet, it was impossible to pay these prices. So after a couple of stormy meetings, the parties parted. The next morning there appeared, in huge white letters chalked on the side of the flume, the words, "Dried Up." So people decided to move on. Tents were taken down, and the store and the eating house were broken up. The once busy mining bar was deserted. We had to go, too. We later heard that a more sensible mind contrived a way of tapping a river above the bluffs to provide the necessary water, and that, some years after the great failure, much profitable mining was done.

Sarah Royce was very proud of the way that she made her tent home into a "real" home. Many people lived in houses like this for so long that they came to be like home. Tent homes were, considering how often people moved, a sensible sort of home to have. The Royces were able to take their home with them when they moved. The men who ran the restaurant in the picture below would have been able to move on if their business did not take off in this particular town, or if the mining seam ran out, and the town broke up. This photograph was taken in the 1880s, and you can see how prices have fallen, and different food is available. Compare the prices here with the prices in the information box on page 31. Fresh beef and pork were obviously available; indeed, the food seems to consist entirely of meat!

A picture of Helena, a mining town, taken in 1870. The houses are fairly permanent-looking, the streets have signposts, the houses have boarded walkways to make getting around in the winter mud easier. People are beginning to fence off their plots of land, and some walkways, like the one on the right at the front, even have very ornate railings. The doors and windows of at least some of the buildings have glass in them. More building is obviously going on, in the town and just outside it. Women, such as the two ladies meeting in the center of the picture, were said to be the "civilizing influence," that led to many of these developments. Certainly, as more women came to these towns, they became proper communities of settlers, rather than camps of men who felt they would soon be going home rich.

Early in the morning of a very hot day, we were again packed into a wagon, this time with a second one to follow. We headed toward the mountains. We were going to another mining camp, some miles into the foothills. This was, again, reported to be a flourishing town, and we hoped that this time we could set up shop and make our home there. We had looked at the camp before we set out and chose a pretty spot about a mile from the camp to set up our tent. In the morning, we decided that this was, indeed, the place to make our home. But we found that this place was already taken, so we found a similar spot farther from the town, on the road to Sacramento. Here our frame house, which we had brought with us, was set up with the help of some local men. We stretched a bit of awning over the least sheltered side and another piece toward the road. This made the kitchen, where we set up the cookstove on a box to keep it off the ground and tied it to a tree. The table and chairs were set close by, and, considering the season, this was much more comfortable than cooking and eating indoors would have been.

could now use the whole inside of my house as a bedroom and parlor, which made it very spacious. Meanwhile, the older children went about their business of making playhouses, and the baby peeped out of a large, square box that I had carpeted for her. It was a beautiful place but lonely. Because my husband was needed in the store in the camp, I often found myself alone with the children. At first, this was not a problem. The days were long and sunny, and I could work outside or sit and sew in the sun. But the seasons changed, and as my husband began to need to be away overnight, I began to feel it to be a dangerous place to be. I felt I was at the mercy of the local Indians or any passersby. This was brought home to me when two men stopped at the house to ask for water. One of them was a foreigner, with a truly awful and menacing face. They drank the water and left, quite politely, but I could not put that face out of my mind. I knew I was to be alone that night, so I decided to keep guard. I had made, for the hot weather, two "windows" for our house, by ripping the fabric, rolling the seams back, and pinning them. They could then be let down again, like curtains, at night and attached with pins. I did not pin the window that night but let the flaps down and then peeked through the slit to watch the road.

I began to think my fears groundless when I heard a shrill bark that rose to a loud howl. But all it was was a large coyote that sniffed around the house and went on its way. Then I heard definite footsteps along the road. Then a shape, definitely a man, came from the road toward our house, stopped, listened, and then made its way back to the road again. The footsteps began again, then faded away. I decided I had kept guard long enough. I lay down and, exhausted, slept till morning. We were eating breakfast, when there was a tap on the frame of the door. It was a friend we had known in the village by the Bay. He joined us for breakfast, and it turned out that it was he who was responsible for my fright the night before. He had been coming to visit us but had lost his way and arrived late. Seeing the house in darkness, he had decided that he would not disturb us and had gone into the town to spend the night in the public house. Soon my husband was back, too, and all my fears seemed foolish. But in a few nights I was left alone again, and my fears returned.

One night, I was awakened from sleep by the noise of horses and men and heard one say to the other, "I know she's alone. Her husband said he would be gone two days this morning." I was terrified. Then my name was called. They were men from the town who were seeking a friend who was lost. They had been discussing whether their calling would frighten me! Well, they had. This kind of incident was not agreeable. We discussed the matter and decided that we should move into the town itself.

CHAPTER 11

Home at Last!

WHAT NEXT?

Sarah Royce and her family lived in this area, Grass Valley, until 1866. It was here that they had a fourth child, Josiah. Sarah Royce found that there was no local school to send the children to. She promptly started one in her own home, providing a wide education for her children and many others.

When they moved back to San Francisco in 1866, her teaching had been good enough for Josiah to sail through the state school system, and to study at a university. He went to Germany in 1875 to study theology. He returned to the United States to become a lecturer at Harvard University. The book of Sarah Royce's memories that Josiah produced does not record what happened to her three girls.

So, in early fall, I said farewell to the canvas house. I never saw it again. We moved into the mining town. Here we lived in a little frame cottage that, while it was not in the bustling center of the town, was close enough to others for me to feel safe and protected. There were not many families in the town itself, but there were two or three with whom we soon got acquainted.

Our neighbors, hearing me playing on the melodeon, soon formed the habit of dropping in on certain evenings of the week to "have a sing," as they put it. After we had been there for a while, we were visited by a minister who lived a few miles off. We talked to him about the need for a church in the town and the impossibility of fixing anything quickly, so it was arranged that he would preach in our living room, which was, apart from the barroom of the tavern down in the ravine, quite the largest room in the town. He had appointments in several towns to do this, so he could not come to us each week — others had to be allowed their turn, too. But he managed to come once every two weeks, which was better than we had been used to for some time. Some of the miners would make friendly fun of us, making jokes about the "psalm singing" in our house. Yet the remarks were not made in any unpleasant way. We certainly managed to gather a good congregation, once the services became known — enough to crowd the room pretty well and tax our ingenuity to seat everyone, even with chairs that we borrowed from our neighbors.

Talking of the reaction of the miners to our religion makes me remember an interesting thing about their reaction (and that of miners in other places, too, so I have heard) to people who were in earnest in religion. They seemed to feel both curiosity and respect. They thought it was a good thing to have such people living in their towns, to lend them some kind of moral tone, unless, of course, such people were to try to encourage them to attend church, in which case they took fright and avoided them altogether.

But we did not have the opportunity to hold many services or even form many new friends. In the spring, we discussed our situation and decided on yet another removal. The store was doing well, yet it was felt that it would do better if set up in a larger, more established mining community. We hoped that this would be our last removal; indeed, I was heartily sick by this time of moving on. It seemed that no sooner did we begin to settle in a place than it was time to move on. I could not but feel that our last two moves, especially to the lonely house on the roadway, had not been for the better, considering how good our life had been on the Bay. Yet I made up my mind to face what was to come cheerfully and with a good heart, for I did not blame my husband for his urge to better himself.

This new mining town was one of the largest and most pleasant of the mining towns that were set quite high up in the Sierra Nevada Mountains. It was higher than Weaverville, our first California dwelling place. So having worked our way all the way down the mountains to the Bay, we had come full circle into the mountains.

We made contact, almost at once, with a number of very good Christian people. There were three churches in the town, all well attended, and a Sunday school for the children. There was also a good-sized public school and one or two social and beneficial societies. Here I seemed to find a natural resting place. We lived in that town for some twelve years, either in the town or close on its outskirts, for we still changed homes from time to time, if not towns. We were accepted, long-term inhabitants.

From the security of our new home, we watched as California passed through various stages and dangers. There was the Vigilance Committee movement, which spread from San Francisco right across the state, even affecting us in our mountaintop aerie. The Frazer River excitement set many people moving on. Washoe fever swept through the state, closely followed by the awful roar of Civil War from the mouths of cannons on the Atlantic shore. But good things swept in, too, including the Overland Railroad, which finally joined the state to the rest of America with ease. We, too, were, after all our travels, at last at ease.

The town of Bodie, California, once a mining town, as it is today. In the center of the town, there is a church tower. Many of these mining towns, once they began to get settled, put up a church. The lives of the more "godly" local citizens would revolve around the church.

Glossary

All definitions refer to Sarah Royce's use of the word in the 1850s.

alkali   a chemical that would make grass and water poisonous.

bar   a kind of barrier.

bluff   a piece of land that has a steep, wide face.

bound   heading for a certain place.

cholera   a sickness, carried by water that is not pure. It causes vomiting and diarrhea and can lead to death if not treated in time.

companies   This has two meanings here:

1. groups of people. Some companies heading west organized themselves in a military way, like Sarah Royce's group. Other companies just traveled together, with no rules laid down. Companies with rules usually managed better.

2. business companies formed by a number of people for a particular job — running a mine, building a dam, or any other large job that a small group would not have the skills or number of people to do.

contagion   the spread of a disease from one body to another.

corral   a place to keep animals, usually cows or horses, shut up safely.

cradles   machines used in mining that mechanically rock soil and water together. The soil is washed away. If there is any gold in with the soil, it will be heavier than soil, so it will sink to the bottom of the cradle. It can be taken out once all the soil has gone.

flats   level areas of ground.

flume   a man-made channel to carry water.

gold pans   shallow, round basins used to separate soil and gold. Water is swirled around in the pan, carrying off the soil. The gold, which is heavier, will sink to the bottom.

impassable   not capable of being traveled, crossed, or surmounted.

Indian Agency   when the United States Government made treaties with the Indians, these treaties often divided up the land the Indians were living on. Part of that land, usually the worst part, was for the Indians to live in. It was called a Reservation, and the Indians were expected to stay in that area. To make sure they did, Indian Agencies were set up on the Reservations. The Agent was supposed to teach the Indians to farm, make sure they stayed on the Reservation, keep the white people off it, and keep traders from cheating the Indians or selling them alcohol.

isthmus   a very narrow piece of land that joins two larger parts together.

melodeon   a small organ (a musical instrument like a piano, which has air pumped through pipes to make the noise), often used in church because the sound is deeper than that of a piano.

Mormons   a religious group, the Church of Jesus Christ of Latter-day Saints, set up by Joseph Smith in 1830. (See box on page 16.)

outfit   everything the travelers were taking with them, from small things to the wagon and the animals. It does not usually mean the people, too, but it can.

arley a conversation between members of two groups that are fighting or, at least, not friendly.

arty a group of people.

astor a churchman; usually in a nonconformist Protestant church that believes in simple services.

ilfering stealing things that are of little value.

lacer a word used for gold that can be found close to the surface of the ground, usually on the beds of rivers or streams. Placer was what most of the small groups or single men of the forty-niners mined. They did not have the skills or the manpower to dig deep mines.

lateau a flat area of land, usually high up, so it can be reached only by steep land.

lush cloth, usually cotton or silk, that has a soft surface made by looping and then cutting the threads in weaving (like velvet, but with longer threads).

rairie flat grasslands, usually treeless.

recipitous very steep.

rovisions supplies of food and drink.

uicksand loose, wet sand. It opens up and swallows anything that weighs on it. Heavy objects sink more quickly.

rakes cracked trunks of trees.

nanty a home made from bits and pieces collected from the area, such as wood logs or branches.

de half of the body of the animal — in this case, a pig.

pasms violent, uncontrollable movements that shake the whole body.

treet grading leveling out streets to avoid bumps and potholes. Grading was done by dragging a heavy metal frame over the roads. The frame was usually pulled by horses.

weet potato a sort of potato from South America that is sweeter than an ordinary potato.

arantula word used for several types of large spiders. They bite, and the bite can be poisonous.

eam a group of animals working together.

enements houses with several rooms or groups of rooms that are owned by one family and rented out.

nicket a group of bushes and trees growing close together.

ongue the wooden pole on the front of the wagon that the animals are attached to so they can pull it.

urbid thick and muddy.

nyoked freed from the yoke.

rashed out getting gold by the process of panning (*see* **gold pans**).

oke **This has two meanings here:**
1. a device to team up two animals together to work. Usually made of wood, it fit across the tongue of the wagon, joining an animal on either side of it and holding them there, usually by chains that went under their necks. (See picture on page 6.)
2. the animals that were attached together as a pair to work.

Index

Numbers in *italic* type refer to captions and pictures; numbers in **bold** type refer to information boxes.

Selections and additional material ©Heinemann Educational 199